DATE DUE

BRODART, CO.   Cat. No. 23-221-003

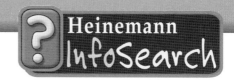

SCIENCE ANSWERS
Classification
FROM MAMMALS TO FUNGI

Heinemann Library
Chicago, Illinois

Louise and Richard Spilsbury

Design: Richard Parker and Celia Floyd
Illustrations: Wooden Ark
Picture Research: Rebecca Sodergren
 and Pete Morris
Originated by Dot Gradations Ltd.
Printed in China by WKT
 Company Limited

08 07 06 05 04
10 9 8 7 6 5 4 3 2 1

**Library of Congress Cataloging-in-
Publication Data**
Spilsbury, Louise.
  Classification : from mammals to fungi /
Louise Spilsbury and Richard Spilsbury.
     p. cm. -- (Science answers)
Includes bibliographical references and
index.
ISBN 1-4034-4763-2 (lib. bdg.) -- ISBN 1-
4034-5509-0 (pbk.)
1. Biology--Classification--Juvenile
literature. [1.
Biology--Classification.] I. Spilsbury,
Richard, 1963- II. Title. III.
Series.
  QH83.S735 2004
  578'.01'2--dc22

                              2003025624

Acknowledgments
The author and publishers are grateful to
the following for permission to reproduce
copyright material:

p.4 Gray Hardel/Corbis; p.6 Norbert
Wu/NHPA; pp.7, 19 Tudor Photography/
Harcourt Education Ltd.; p.8 ZEFA; p.9
Dr. Tony Brain & Dr. David Parker/Science
Photo Library; p.10 Eric Grave/Science
Photo Library; p.11 Jan Hinsch/Science
Photo Library; p.12 Eye of Science/Science
Photo Library; p.13 Chris Mattison/FLPA;
p.14 Tudor Photography; p.15 David
Woodfall/NHPA; pp.16, 22, 26 Stephen
Dalton/NHPA; p.17 G. J. Cambridge/NHPA;
p.18 Corbis; p.20 Christopher Ratier/NHPA;
p.21 Trevor McDonald/NHPA; p.23 ANT
Photo Library/NHPA; p.24 Claude
Nuridsany & Marie Perennou/SPL; p.25
Daniel Heuclin/NHPA; p.27 Daryl
Balfour/NHPA; p.28 Carl Linnaeus/Science
Photo Library; p.29 Rudiger
Lehnen/Science Photo Library.

Cover photograph reproduced with
permission of P. Hartman/FLPA.

Every effort has been made to contact
copyright holders of any material
reproduced in this book. Any omissions
will be rectified in subsequent printings
if notice is given to the publisher.

Some words are shown in
bold, **like this.** You can find
out what they mean by
looking in the glossary.

Contents

About the activities

This book contains some sections called Science Answers. Each one describes an activity that you can try yourself. There are some simple safety rules to follow when doing an experiment:
- Ask an adult to help with any cutting that uses a sharp knife.
- Always wash your hands with soap after handling plant or animal material.

Materials you will use

Most of the activities in this book can be done with objects that you can find in your own home. You might also need to buy some items from a grocery store. You will also need a pencil and paper to record results.

What Is Classification?

Classification is the way people make sense of the world. When people classify, they arrange things into groups according to their similarities and differences. For example, you classify when you sort toys into boxes or put books away in alphabetical order in a library.

Classifying life

Living things have several **life processes** in common such as growth, **respiration,** and **reproduction.** But living things can be as different as a cactus and a shark. People classify living things partly based on their appearance. For example, any animal with feathers is a bird. However, although some creatures such as birds and bats look similar in shape, they are very different. This is why we classify partly based on how these things live. For example, birds lay eggs while bats do not. Some differences between **organisms** are very small, so classification can be difficult.

A variety of life

There is a huge variety of living organisms in nature. Sometimes it is possible to find many different kinds of life in the same place. For example, tropical forests and coral reefs are homes to many different kinds of living things. Classifying and naming the different living things on Earth is called taxonomy.

Kingdoms of life

There are an estimated ten million different **species** of living things on Earth. Up until the 20th century, scientists divided organisms into two big groups, called **kingdoms.** Today most scientists agree that living things should be classified into five kingdoms. These are named monera, protists, fungi, plants, and animals. The members of each kingdom share similar features.

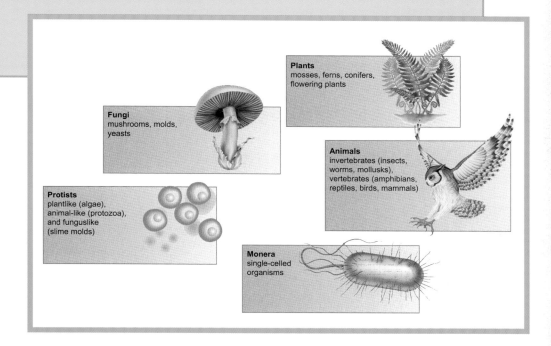

Plants
mosses, ferns, conifers, flowering plants

Fungi
mushrooms, molds, yeasts

Animals
invertebrates (insects, worms, mollusks), vertebrates (amphibians, reptiles, birds, mammals)

Protists
plantlike (algae), animal-like (protozoa), and funguslike (slime molds)

Monera
single-celled organisms

Classification over time

Early humans classified the plants or animals they found as either safe or harmful. Over 2,300 years ago, the Greek philosopher Aristotle classified some organisms by their insides. For example, he classified organisms by whether they had blood or not and how they behaved. In the 18th century, the Swedish **botanist** Carolus Linnaeus developed a system for classifying any living thing. Scientists today classify using Linnaeus's system plus more recent information, such as the kinds of **cells** inside an organism's body.

Classification groupings

Within each **kingdom, organisms** are divided up into large subgroups called **phyla.** Each phylum is divided into smaller groups with shared features called classes. Classes are divided into smaller groups called orders, orders are divided into families, families are divided into **genera,** and genera into **species.** A species is a single kind of organism. The members of a species are very similar and can usually **reproduce** together.

Universal species

Mountain lion, puma, and *cougar* are different names for the same species of big cat. To avoid this kind of confusion, every species is given a Latin name. This language was widely understood when Linnaeus developed his classification system. *Felis concolor* is the Latin name for what people call mountain lions, pumas, and cougars. *Felis* is the genus and *concolor* is the individual species name.

Similar but not the same

Some animals, such as dolphins and fish, look similar but are classified into different groups. Although this bottlenose dolphin lives in water and looks sort of like a fish, it is actually a mammal like humans and dogs.

ACTIVITY: Sorting into groups

EQUIPMENT

A mixed box of differently sized, shaped, and colored candies; a bag of peanuts in the shells; two large sheets of paper; pens

STEPS

1. Take a sheet of paper and put the candies on it.
2. Divide the candies into groups containing similar features. You can sort them by color, shape, or whether they are hard or soft.
3. Draw circles around the different groups. Some candies can fall into more than one group. With these candies, make a separate pile located in between the two piles they could belong to.
4. Repeat steps 1 and 2 with the peanuts. You may have to use different features to sort them such as length. Then break open each peanut shell. Sort them by the number of peanuts inside each shell.

EXPLANATION

Candies are easier to classify than peanuts because their differences and similarities are more obvious. Sometimes it is possible to classify things using features that cannot be seen. This is why scientists often have to dissect animals to see the bones and organs.

7

What Are Monera?

Monera make up one the five **kingdoms.** Most monera are bacteria. Bacteria are the simplest living things on Earth. Billions of them live in water, soil, air, and on or in other **organisms.** Bacteria are classified by the shapes of their **cells.** For example, some bacteria are round, some are shaped like rods, and others are look like corkscrews.

Simple cells

Cells are the building blocks of all living things. Most cells contain a distinct part called a **nucleus** that helps control the **life processes** in the cell. Bacteria are classified together partly because they have no nucleus. Bacteria usually live as single cells or chains of identical cells.

Helpful bacteria

Many animals depend on bacteria in their stomachs to help them **digest** food. Humans have bacteria in their stomachs that help with digestion. Yogurt has the same kind of bacteria that live in human stomachs. It is called *Lactobacillus acidophilus.* It protects our digestive tract and helps in digestion. Other bacteria are used to make foods such as cheese, as well as medicines.

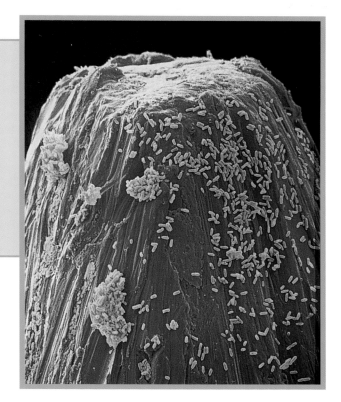

Harmful bacteria

Some bacteria are harmful to other organisms. They affect life processes, usually by producing damaging chemicals. Bacteria **reproduce** very quickly in the right conditions. This means that sicknesses and diseases that are caused by bacteria can spread quickly.

Cyanobacteria

Cyanobacteria are a type of bacteria that has existed for billions of years. They use energy from sunlight to make their own food. Plants also use this process, which is called **photosynthesis.**

Cyanobacteria often live in groups called colonies. Some colonies live around the roots of plants where they help plants get **nutrients.** Some cyanobacteria live on bare, wet rock or concrete. Others live in extreme conditions such as hot springs. Although the water there is rich in nutrients, it can also be as hot as 165 °F (75 °C). In contrast, red cyanobacteria live in the freezing snows of Antarctica.

What Are Protists?

The protist **kingdom** is made up of single-**celled organisms** that can only be seen under a microscope and live in water. Protists differ from bacteria because they have distinct **nuclei.**

Some protists move around

Some protists are like small animals because they move around to find and consume food instead of making it themselves as plants do. Some protists, such as amoebas, move by stretching out part of their cell wall. Their liquid body flows into the new space created. Others have a long hair that they wave back and forth to swim along like fish.

Protists have different ways of getting food. *Vorticella* has an opening in the top of its cell that is surrounded by small hairs. When the *Vorticella* beats the hairs in water, it creates a kind of whirlpool that funnels floating food into its body.

Catching a meal

Amoebas eat bacteria and protists. They move around to trap their **prey** before **digesting** it. In this photograph an amoeba is surrounding its prey, a protist called a paramecium. When the prey is totally surrounded, it will be swallowed and digested inside the amoeba.

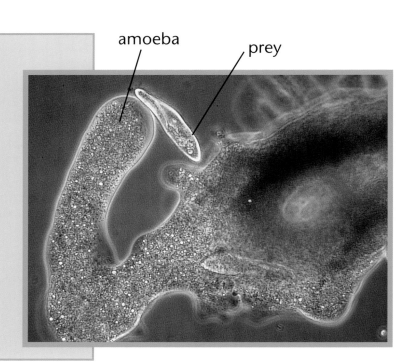

amoeba

prey

Protists that make their own food

Some protists are like plants because they produce their own food using **photosynthesis.** Protists in the world's oceans make up the major part of **plankton. Oxygen** is created as a waste product of photosynthesis by these protists. Marine animals need this oxygen to survive. Plankton is also an important food source for fish and other animals that live in the ocean.

Diatoms are protists with two hard shells that look like glass. The shells form boxes around the diatoms in different shapes such as stars or circles.

Colorful creatures

There are over 10,000 different **species** of protists. Each diatom species has a different pattern, color, and shape.

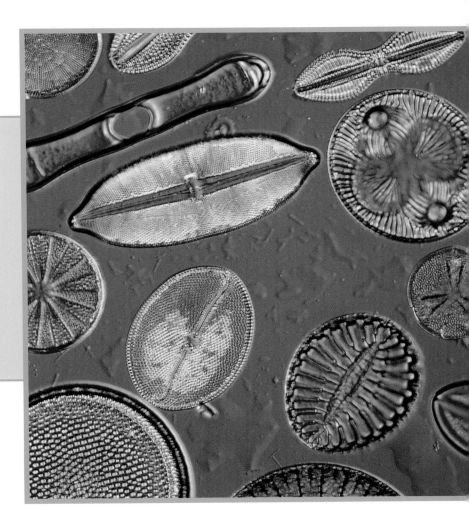

What Are Fungi?

The fungi **kingdom** groups together **organisms** such as mushrooms, toadstools, and yeast. Yeasts, mildews, and molds are small, single-**celled** fungi. Larger fungi such as mushrooms, puffballs, and toadstools are made up of many different cells.

Hidden fungi

Many fungi are made up of a network of cottonlike threads called **hyphae.** Hyphae grow through materials such as damp soil and wood. The hyphae make chemicals that break down the soil and wood. The hyphae then take in the released **nutrients.**

Hyphae are usually hidden. The parts of fungi that you can see are used to **reproduce** using **spores.** Spores are like small, tough seeds. The thin flaps on the underside of a mushroom's wide cap are where the spores are made. When the spores are ripe, they may fall, blow, or wash away to a place with the right growing conditions where they can develop into new fungi.

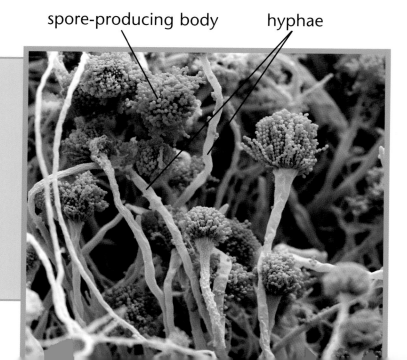

spore-producing body   hyphae

Parts of a fungus

This magnified photo of the fungus *Aspergillus fumigatus* shows its structure. It is made up of threadlike hyphae and spore-producing bodies.

Decomposers and helpers

Some fungi break down dead organisms. This is called **decomposition.** These fungi feed on dead wood and leaves, which are full of useful nutrients. They absorb some of the nutrients and the rest wash into the ground. This makes the soil fertile, helping different plants grow.

Tree recycling

Fungi are very important decomposers of dead organisms. Fungi remove nutrients from dead organisms and change them into a form that other living organisms can use. This picture shows shelf fungi growing on a fallen tree in a forest in Costa Rica.

Many fungi grow hyphae into and among tree roots. Some of the nutrients that their hyphae take in from the soil enter the trees' roots as well. In return, some of the sugar in the roots, which the trees make by **photosynthesis,** is absorbed by the hyphae. This kind of relationship that benefits both living things is called **mutualism.**

No benefit

Some fungi are **parasites.** Parasites feed on other living things without providing anything useful in return. For example, athlete's foot is caused by a fungus that lives on human skin. It makes the skin flake and itch.

What Are Plants?

Plants make up one of the best-known **kingdoms** of living things. All plants can make their own food. They do this by **photosynthesis.** In this process, plants use energy from sunlight to combine water and **carbon dioxide** to create sugars. Plants' ability to produce their own food is what sets them apart from the other kingdoms of living things.

Kinds of plants

Even though all plants photosynthesize, there are many different kinds of plants. The simplest way of grouping them is to look at their structures. Plants differ in the way they take in water and **nutrients.** They can be grouped by whether they are **vascular** or **nonvascular.**

Parts of a vascular flowering plant

Photosynthesis happens mostly in plant leaves. The flowers are used for **reproduction.** They make seeds that are stored in fruits. Stems hold up the other parts of the plant. Roots fix the plant in the ground and take in water and nutrients from the soil.

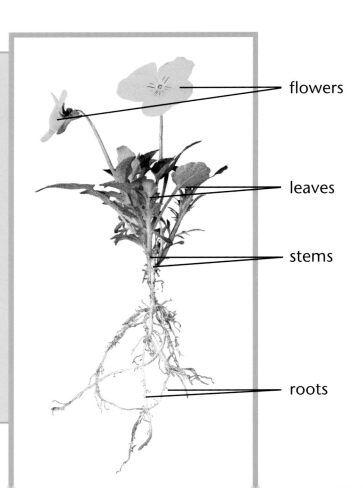

flowers

leaves

stems

roots

14

Vascular plants

Vascular plants move water, nutrients, and food around their bodies in a series of tubes. They take in water and **dissolved** nutrients from the soil through their roots. The water is taken from the roots through tubes to the stems and leaves. Sugars that are made in the leaves are then carried to other parts of the plant by tubes. The tubes in vascular plants are connected together like the blood vessels inside the human body.

Plant tubes

Vascular plants have two kinds of tubes. Xylem tubes carry water and nutrients from the roots to the other parts of the plant. Phloem tubes carry the sugars made in the leaves to the other parts of the plant.

Vascular heights

Most of the plants in the world are vascular plants. These beech trees are vascular plants. They can grow tall because their tubes carry water and nutrients up and down the plant.

Vascular plant groups

Vascular plants can be divided into three different groups: flowering plants; conifers; and ferns and their relatives, the club mosses and horsetails. Flowering plants **reproduce** using seeds made in flowers. Conifers make seeds, too, but in **cones** instead of flowers. The ferns and their relatives reproduce using **spores.**

Flowers

For a seed to grow in a flowering plant, **pollen** from the male part of a flower has to join with an egg in the female part. This is called **pollination.** The female part can be in the same flower or in a different flower. Some flowers attract insects or birds to eat their **nectar.** As they feed, the visitors also pick up pollen that they transfer to other flowers. Other flowering plants use the wind to spread their pollen to other plants.

Smelly flowers

Honeysuckle flowers smell strongest in the evenings. Their smell attracts moths, which fly at night. The moths feed on the honeysuckle nectar and transfer pollen to other flowers.

Conifers

Most conifers have leaves shaped like needles. Conifers are often called **evergreens.** They gradually shed and replace their needles year round so that they always look green. Conifers have two types of cones on their branches that are used for reproduction. The smaller male cones produce pollen that blows onto larger female cones. Once pollinated, seeds develop inside the female cones. These cones fall or open up to release the seeds when they are ready.

Fern spores

The patches on the undersides of these fern fronds are clusters of spores. The spores may grow into new fern plants when they fall to the ground.

Ferns, club mosses, and horsetails

The plants in this third group of vascular plants reproduce using spores. Their water-carrying tubes are found in the walls of their hollow stems. There are about 12,500 different **species** of ferns. Ferns have leaflike parts called fronds. Most of these fronds grow from underground stems. Club mosses are not really mosses, but they grow close to the ground like mosses do. Horsetails have circles of thin leaves around their stems.

Nonvascular plants

Nonvascular plants do not have tubes. They usually get the water and **nutrients** they need by growing in damp places. The different parts of the plants, such as leaves, take in the water they need from their surroundings.

Nonvascular plants can be divided into two groups: mosses and liverworts are one group, and algae are the other group. In the woodland in this picture, mosses grow on the trees and algae live in the water.

Mosses and liverworts

Mosses and liverworts have leaves, stems, and roots. They live on damp walls, roofs, rocks, and on fallen trees. Moss grows in groups, forming spongy, green cushions. Liverworts also live together in groups and they have small, flat, green leaves. Both **reproduce** using **spores.**

Algae

Algae have no leaves, stems, or roots. Some algae consist of a single **cell.** Other algae, such as seaweed, have large fronds. Small algae reproduce by dividing cells. Larger algae such as kelp reproduce using spores.

ACTIVITY: Leaf classification

EQUIPMENT
Ten different tree leaves, which can be fallen leaves, cuttings given by someone with a garden, or photos of leaves on trees; paper; pencil

STEPS
1. Study the leaves to see what differences and similarities they have. Are the leaves like small, pointed scales? Are they needle-shaped or wide? Are they simple leaves or groups of smaller leaves on one stalk?
2. Sort the leaves into groups according to the differences you identify. Write down the details of the different groups. You can even draw some of the leaf shapes to study the differences.

EXPLANATION
Trees are classified partly according to leaf shape. Trees with needle-like or scale leaves are conifers. For example, pine trees have leaves shaped like needles. Cedar trees have leaves shaped like scales. Other leaves have broad shapes. Single broad leaves such as oak or holly are called simple leaves. Leaves made up of groups of

smaller leaves are called compound leaves. Compound leaves are found on trees such as ash. Use a tree identification book to identify tree **species** more closely.

What Are Animals?

The animal **kingdom** groups together **organisms** as different as whales and jellyfish. Even though they can be very different, all animals are made of many **cells** and get all the energy they need to live by consuming food. Most animals can move at some stage in their life. Many animals sense and react to the world using nerves and muscles controlled by a brain.

Kinds of animals

Animals are usually grouped based on how they support and protect their bodies. Most **species** of animals in the world are **invertebrates,** which have no internal bony skeleton. Invertebrates have other ways to keep their body shape. For example, worms have spaces inside their bodies that are filled with fluids. Crabs have a hard outer shell.

Only about three percent of all animals are **vertebrates.** These animals have backbones and internal skeletons. There are five classes of vertebrates: fish, reptiles, amphibians, birds, and mammals.

Animal consumers

Most animals get food by consuming other organisms. Some of them, like this cheetah, rely on speed to catch their **prey.**

Which Animals Are Invertebrates?

Invertebrates range in size from microscopic worms to giant squids as long as a bus. They are divided into around 30 **phyla.** These include sea urchins, sea stars, worms, sponges, and the following groups.

Mollusks

Squid, octopuses, clams, and mussels are all mollusks. Many mollusks have a rough tongue for grating food. Mollusks such as snails live inside shells that protect their bodies. Slugs have a slimy outer skin.

Sea anemones, corals, and jellyfish

These invertebrates belong to one group because they have special stinging cells on their **tentacles** to catch food and protect themselves from attack. Corals live together in vast groups on the sea floor. The chalky or rubbery skeletons that corals live in are what make up reefs.

How do anemones feed?

Sea anemones can attach themselves to rocks or coral. Their tentacles are arranged in a ring around their mouths. They wait for their food to swim by, sting it with their tentacles, and push it into their mouths.

21

Arthropods

Arthropods are **invertebrates** such as insects, millipedes, lobsters, and scorpions. They have tough **exoskeletons** on the outsides of their bodies. Their bodies are divided into sections and their legs have joints so that they can bend. As arthropods get bigger, they grow out of their exoskeletons. They have to **molt** to get rid of the old exoskeleton and replace it with a new, bigger one.

Deadly tails

Scorpions use the stingers on their tails to inject poison into their prey. This stops the prey from moving as the scorpion eats it alive.

Arthropod classification

One way of classifying arthropods is by the number of body parts or legs that they have. For example, all adult insects have three body sections and six legs. Spiders and scorpions both have two body sections and eight legs, but differ in how they catch **prey.** Spiders make sticky webs to catch their prey. Scorpions use large claws at the front of their legs and stingers on their tails.

How Are Fish and Frogs Different?

Fish and frogs are both **vertebrates** that hatch from soft eggs in water. Fish spend their whole lives in water. Frogs are amphibians. Amphibians spend the early part of their lives in water but live mainly on land as adults.

Fish live their whole lives in water

Fish live in the oceans, rivers, and lakes. Some fish move between oceans and rivers. Fish breathe using their gills, which take in **oxygen** from the water. Fish swim by moving their tails from side to side and using their fins for control. Fish skin is usually covered with scales that fit together like the shingles on a roof. Young fish eat small plants, insect eggs, or **larvae.** Adult fish eat **plankton,** plants, smaller fish, or other animals.

Fishy facts

There are many different kinds of fish in the world. The dwarf pygmy goby fish from the Philippines is only 0.5 inches (13 millimeters) long when fully grown. On the other hand, whale sharks like this one measure as much as 60 feet (19 meters) long.

Amphibians

Frogs, toads, newts, and salamanders are all amphibians. Young amphibians that hatch from eggs are called **larvae.** They look completely different from adult amphibians. As larvae develop, they undergo huge changes in a process called **metamorphosis.** Adult amphibians have soft, moist skin without scales. They are **cold-blooded,** which means that their bodies stay the same temperature as their surroundings. However, amphibians can warm up by lying in the sun.

Frog metamorphosis

Female frogs lay hundreds of eggs underwater. Tadpoles hatch out of these eggs. Tadpoles have long tails for swimming, and they breathe using gills. They eat pieces of plants using tiny teeth. As they grow, tadpoles develop legs so they can walk on land. Their tails get much smaller (notice the short tail on this frog in the photograph) until they have no tails at all. About four months after hatching, young frogs leave the water to live on land. Adult frogs have lungs so that they can breathe air. They eat small insects that they catch with a sticky tongue.

What Are Reptiles and Birds?

There are many similarities between reptiles and birds. To **reproduce,** both kinds of animals lay eggs on land, usually in nests. Reptiles lay leathery eggs while birds lay hard eggs. The eggs' shells protect the babies inside from drying up. This allows reptiles and birds to live in drier places than animals such as amphibians. There are also some important differences between reptiles and birds.

Scaly reptiles

Most reptiles have skin covered with scales and their mouths have teeth. There are four different groups of reptiles. Snakes have long bodies and no legs. Crocodiles and alligators have long jaws, long tails, and short legs. Lizards are similar to crocodiles and alligators, but they are much smaller and have shorter heads. Turtles and tortoises have bodies protected by bony shells.

From small to big

When reptiles such as this baby grass snake hatch out of their leathery eggs, they look like tiny versions of their parents. Most reptiles can get food and protect themselves right away.

Birds have feathers

Birds are the only living things that have skin covered with feathers. All birds have wings, which most **species** use for flying. Birds do not have teeth. They catch their food using a hard beak or the claws on their feet. Birds usually lay their eggs in nests. There is a huge variety of birds on Earth, from hummingbirds only two inches (five centimeters) long, to ostriches that are almost nine feet (three meters) tall.

Finding food

Birds eat a variety of foods and find it in different ways. Many birds feed during the day, but owls have large eyes and hunt at night for small animals such as mice. Hummingbirds beat their wings quickly to hover over flowers as they lap up **nectar** with their long tongues. Pelicans have a pouchlike throat that they use to scoop up fish from the water.

Where do birds live?

Birds live in all parts of the world. This colorful macaw lives in the Amazonian rain forest in South America.

How Are Mammals Classified?

Mammals can look as different as giraffes, whales, and humans. However, all mammals have a number of things in common.

Mammals are all **vertebrates** that have hair on some or all of their bodies. They are **warm-blooded,** which means that they can keep the same inside temperature whether it is hot or cold outside. All mammals breathe air through lungs. Female mammals feed their babies milk that their own bodies make.

Mother's milk

Most baby mammals, like this young giraffe, suckle milk from teats on the mother's belly or chest.

Unusual mammals

Most mammal babies develop inside their mothers for a period of time. However, female marsupials such as kangaroos and opossums give birth to small, undeveloped young. Their young usually develop in a pouch on the mother's belly. Platypuses are mammals that lay eggs. After they hatch, platypus babies drink their mothers' milk.

Aristotle (384–322 B.C.E.)

Aristotle was a teacher, writer, and philosopher in Ancient Greece. His new ways of thinking influenced many different areas of study, including biology. Aristotle was the first person to classify animals by how they lived or by how they were made up. For example, Aristotle figured out that dolphins are not fish, even though they look similar. His work influenced scientists for hundreds of years after his death.

Carolus Linnaeus (1707–1778)

Linnaeus (pictured here) was a Swedish **botanist.** He published the book *Systema Naturae,* which was a universal system for classifying life on Earth. It could be used by any scientist who could speak or read Latin. This included his way of giving any **organism** a double name, showing its **genus** and its **species.** Linnaeus's system is still used today.

Amazing Facts

- The chemical that keeps the feathers of African flamingos pink comes from the algae they eat.

- The green color of slow-moving mammals called sloths comes from the algae that live in their fur!

- One fungus in Oregon covers over six square miles (ten square kilometers) beneath the pine forest floor. The fungus may have lived in this place for over 8,000 years.

- There are over half a million beetle species. That is one in every four animal species on Earth.

- Although there are only 8,000 ant species, there are so many individual ants that together they weigh one tenth of all animals put together!

- Some ocean snails live at depths of 2.5 miles (4 kilometers).

- The giant clam (below) can reach 5 feet (1.5 meters) long. It can weigh over 440 pounds (200 kilograms).

Glossary

botanist   plant scientist

carbon dioxide   gas found in small amounts in air. Plants use it for photosynthesis and animals breathe it out.

cell   building block of living things that can only be seen with a microscope. Most plants and animals are made up of millions of cells.

cold-blooded   animal that has no automatic control over its body temperature. Cold-blooded animals stay the same temperature as their surroundings.

cone   dry fruit in which conifer seeds develop. Cones are often egg-shaped with overlapping woody scales.

decomposition   breaking down chemically, or rotting

digest   break down food into nutrients that an organism can use

dissolve   mix together with a liquid

evergreen   tree that is always losing and replacing a few leaves throughout the year

exoskeleton   hard covering on the outside of an arthropod's body

genus (more than one are genera)   classification grouping. Each genus is divided into species.

hypha (more than one are hyphae)   threadlike part that a fungus uses to take in nutrients

invertebrate   animal without a backbone

kingdom   one of the five groups that living things are divided into

larva (more than one are larvae)   young that looks very different from its parents and must undergo changes before it becomes an adult

life process   characteristic that most living things have

metamorphosis   change in body shape that happens in some kinds of organisms as they grow

molt   shed feathers, hair, or skin

mutualism   partnership between two living things from which both members benefit

nectar   sugary liquid that plants make in their flowers to attract insects and birds

nonvascular   does not have veins or tubes in its body

nucleus (more than one are nuclei)   part of a cell that helps control the life processes within the cell

nutrient   chemical that plants and animals need in order to live

organism   living thing

oxygen   gas in the air which many living things need in order to survive

parasite   organism that lives on or in another living thing and takes food from it without giving any benefit in return

photosynthesis   process by which plants make their own food using water, carbon dioxide, and energy from sunlight

phylum (more than one are phyla)   classification grouping. Each phylum is divided into classes.

plankton   group of microscopic organisms that live in the surface waters of the oceans

pollen   small, dustlike particle that contains male sex cells

pollinate   place pollen on the female part of a flower

prey   animal that is caught and eaten by another animal

reproduce   make young

respiration   process by which living things release energy from their food

species   group of organisms that have similar characteristics

spore   small, seedlike object that some fungi and molds use to reproduce

tentacle   long, thin feeler that sticks out of an organism's body

vascular   has veins or tubes in its body

vertebrate   animal with a backbone

warm-blooded   animal that can keep the same temperature inside its body when the outside temperature changes

More Books to Read

Pascoe, Elaine. *Animals Without Backbones*. New York: Rosen Publishing, 2003.

Solway, Andrew. *Classifying Mammals*. Chicago: Heinemann Library, 2003.

Spilsbury, Louise and Richard Spilsbury. *Plant Classification*. Chicago: Heinemann Library, 2003.

Index